ANDRÉ PREVIN

VIOLIN CONCERTO

("Anne-Sophie")

for Violin and Piano

I. Moderato
II. Cadenza - Slowly
III. Andante
    (from a train in Germany)

ED 4149
First printing: February 2004

ISBN 0-634-03701-3

G. SCHIRMER, Inc.

DISTRIBUTED BY
HAL•LEONARD®
CORPORATION
7777 W. BLUEMOUND RD. P.O. BOX 13819 MILWAUKEE, WI 53213

This work was commissioned by the Boston Symphony Orchestra.
The premiere took place March 14, 2002 by the Boston Symphony Orchestra,
with Anne-Sophie Mutter, violin, conducted by the composer.
A recording by the same artists is available on Deutsche Grammophon, CD 474 500-2

André Previn composed his Violin Concerto for Anne-Sophie Mutter on a commission from the Boston Symphony Orchestra, writing it over the course of four months, completing it in October 2001, and leading the premiere with Mutter and the BSO on March 14, 2002, in Symphony Hall, Boston.

In general, Previn prefers to compose with either a specific artist or a specific occasion in mind. The BSO commission allowed him to write for an orchestra he knows intimately (he has conducted it regularly since 1977) and for a soloist whose playing he also knows well. It was Previn's suggestion that the commissioned work be a violin concerto for Anne-Sophie Mutter, whose playing he admires greatly. When, in 1996, Previn wrote for Mutter, at her request, the violin and piano work *Tango Song and Dance*, he was, in his own words, just "one of her legion of admirers." By the time of the Violin Concerto he had this to say: "I don't know a better musician or violinist, and her technique is flawless. There are certain things she particularly likes, and I was able to give her something that she enjoys performing."

Regarding the work's genesis: In November 1999, while traveling by train in Germany, Previn phoned his New York-based friend, the artist manager Ronald Wilford, waking him with a birthday greeting. The appreciative Wilford continued thinking about the call for days, then suggested to Previn that his new piece reflect that train journey through the country where Previn was born and spent his early childhood. Previn later decided to incorporate into the third movement a German children's song, suggested by Mutter, that he himself had known as a child, "Wenn ich ein Vöglein wär' und auch zwei Flügel hätt', flög' ich zu dir..." ("If I were a bird and had two wings, I'd fly to you..."). That movement, headed "from a train in Germany," became a set of variations on the children's song, the autobiographical connection being further reinforced in the score by an inscription from T.S. Eliot's *Four Quartets*: "We shall not cease from exploration./And the end of all our exploring/will be to arrive where we started/and know the place for the first time."

Previn describes the concerto's first movement as the most lush and conservative of the three, and the second as more barren and acidulous than the rest. Beyond that, he feels that if the music cannot speak for itself, he as a composer has not done his job. His Violin Concerto harks back to early childhood memories, while speaking also of long-standing associations, both personal and professional, with friends and colleagues he holds dear—in short, a testament to relationships past, present, and future.

Marc Mandel

INSTRUMENTATION

3 Flutes (3rd doubling Piccolo)
2 Oboes
English Horn
3 Clarinets in Bb
Bass Clarinet
2 Bassoons
Contrabassoon

4 Horns in F
3 Trumpets in C
3 Trombones

Timpani

Percussion (2 players)
Celesta
Harp

Solo Violin

Strings

duration ca. 39 minutes

Performance material is available on rental from the publisher.
G. Schirmer/AMP Rental and Performance Department
P.O. Box 572
Chester, NY 10918
(845) 469-4699 - phone
(845) 469-7544 - fax
www.schirmer.com

to Anne-Sophie Mutter

VIOLIN CONCERTO
("Anne-Sophie")
I

Edited and fingered by
Anne-Sophie Mutter

André Previn

poco rall.

Suddenly faster

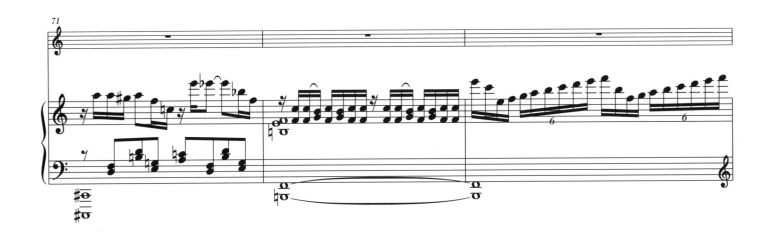

II

III

(from a train in Germany)

Andante

34

Tempo I